A Beautiful Life

Meditation and the Wise Heart

Wusu Dumbuya Jr.

(gpmg)

Global Publishing and Media Group
www.thegpmgroup.com
Alexandria, Virginia

(gpmg)

Global Publishing and Media Group
www.thegpmgroup.com
Alexandria, Virginia

Copyright © 2014 Wusu Dumbuya Jr.
All Rights Reserved.
No part of this book may be reproduced in any manner whatsoever without the written permission of the author or the publisher.

ISBN: 978-0-9860426-2-1 (print)

LCCN:

Printed in the United States of America

For

Zoë

Always exercise compassion and wisdom
towards earth's creations.

Introduction

Meditation allows us to explore on our own. That is where true experience and growth lies. This is why the teachers emphasize meditating alone, without the group setting or guides. It is far better to turn away from dead scriptures and tap directly into our energy. We need to open ourselves to what is unique about our contemporary times, throw off the shackles of outmoded forms and instead adapt to our current spiritual needs. Spirituality and energy assumes that an inner cultivation of character can lead to an
outer resonance.

Self-cultivation is the basis of our energy. Although this energy may be glimpsed in the outer world, we must sharpen our inner sensibilities in order to observe the workings
of the great.

Today there are millions of us exploring meditation for answers we cannot find in our own cultures. In this worthy search, many of us lack an introduction to the spiritual quest. A Beautiful Life: Meditation and the Wise Heart can be your companion. It addresses the awe and devotion of
spiritual life.

The first twelve meditations are guided. Then you will have to draw on your interpretations for the rest of the book. When you succeed in that, books and companions fade away, and the wonder of your spirit and energy is everything.

1

Ablution

*P*urify the inner spirit,

Protect the gods within.

To purify starts all practice. Cleansing of the body- not so to deny the body but so that it is refined.

If we continually eat unhealthy foods, intoxicate ourselves, allow filth to accumulate inside and outside ourselves, the gods within will abandon us in disgust.

Once we are cleansed, we can sense the divine.
We can reach the inner One.

2

Starting

This is the moment we embark,

All auspicious signs are in place.

After purification, we must make a decision.
A decision to self-cultivate. We must connect to our inner self.

Once the decision is made, all things will come to us.
These signs will not be superstitions, they are affirmations.
Pray and the sound of our purpose will reverberate.

3

Devotion

Make crooked thoughts straight,

Make good thoughts flow.

Bring the world into a single point of energy

Gather water, fire, and light.

Devoting faith and commitment to our spiritual path will bring momentum. Nothing will knock us from our track of purpose.

4

Reflection

Moon and sun above water,

Day and night, we sit in solitude.

When water is placid, the moon and sun is reflected perfectly. When we still ourselves, we mirror the divine.

5

Sound

Wind in the heart:

Movement is stillness,

Power is silence.

When listening with the heart and not with
the ear, you can hear feelings. By listening to these
sounds, you enter into supreme purity.

6

Thunder, lightning, in the night.

Growth is with shock.

Duration together with expression,

Appear in the first moment.

Things cannot remain still forever. Storms
May destroy life, but they always prepare way for anew.

7

Forbearance

Mountain, coiled by arctic breath,

Rattling the forests' bones.

Clinging raindrops on branches:

Jeweled adornment flung to earth.

Trees in storms loose their leaves, as some even fall during storms. However, most stand patiently and bear their fortune. No matter what, we should bear both fates patiently while being true to ourselves.

The ant,

Works in all season.

Gathering food and supplies,

Is both action and inaction.

We benefit by working according to seasonal circumstances. Whether it is the time or the method, true labor is half inactivity and half knowing how to let things proceed on their own.

9

Optimism

Clear blue sky,

A promise set in bare branches.

In winter, there are sunny days,

In adulthood, childhood can return.

Sometimes things appear dormant or dead. The rain and snow seem incessant and the nights are even longer. Then all of a sudden, the sky clears to a brilliant blue. The air warms. Gardeners prepare a new stock. We know there will be an end to the cold.

10

Disaster

*W*arm noir night.

Sudden fire.

Chaos.

Destruction.

Disaster strikes at its own time. It is so overwhelming that we can do nothing but accept the state of chaos. It alters the course of our day, work, and our thinking, we can resent disaster but it too shall pass.

11

Healing

Fire seeks its own level,

Water cools.

No matter how extreme our situation, it will change. It cannot continue forever. Natural events balance themselves by seeking their opposites; this process is at the heart of all healing.

12

Shaping

Potter at the wheel,

From centering to finished pot.

Form increases as options decreases,

Softness goes to hardness.

This is how we shape all our situations in
our lives. We must give them a rough sketch
and then throw them down the center of our lives.

13

Absorption

Crimson light through pine shadows,

Setting sun settling in the ocean.

Night follows the sun,

Day replaces the fleeing moon.

14

Positioning

Herron stands in the blue estuary,

Solitary, white, unmoving for hours.

A fish, quick, avian darting;

The prey captured.

Wusu Dumbuya Jr.

15

Time

The river, surging course,

Uninterrupted current.

Headwater, channel, mouth.

Can they be divided?

16

Ordinary

Sea, light, landscape, sky-

There is no language of the holy,

The sacred lies in the ordinary.

17

Cooperation

Cooperation with others;

Perception, tenacity, experience.

Know when to lead and when to follow.

Spectrum

Pure light is all colors,

Therefore, it has no hue

Only when singleness is scattered

Does color appear.

19

Initiative

Let us not be confused

With kaleidoscopic reality.

Using wisdom and courage to act,

Let us not add to the confusion.

20

Happiness

Let us not follow vulgar leaders

Who exploits the fear of death,

And promise the bliss of salvation.

If we are truly happy inside

They will have nothing to offer.

21

Skills

Zither, chess, writing, painting, sword.

These symbolize classical skill.

22

Communication

Movement, objects, speech, and words:

We communicate through gross symbols.

We call them 'objectives'

We still however cannot escape our point of view.

23

Renewal

City on the hill

Untouched land beyond.

A fallow field is

The secret of fertility.

24

Laughter

Hilly village lanes,

Whitewashed sunlit walls.

Cerulean sea.

The laughter of children.

25

Usefulness

An ancient gnarled tree:

Too fibrous for a logger's saw,

Too twisted to fit a carpenter's square,

Outlasts the whole forest.

26

Adoration

Images on the alter,

Or imagined without:

We pray to them,

But do they answer?

Feasting

Feasting is the flame in mid-winter

That kindles the fire of friendship

And strengthens the community.

28

Accountability

A father without a father

Has difficulty balancing.

A master without a master

Is dangerous.

Scars

Markings in dry clay disappear

Only when the clay is soft again.

Scars on the body disappears,

Only when one becomes soft within.

30

Lovemaking

Nocturnal downpour

Wakes the lovers,

And floods the valley.

Wusu Dumbuya Jr.

31

Orientation

Planets orbit the sun,

Forms orbit the mind…

32

Ubiquity

Love is everywhere.

It cannot be kept from the sincere.

33

Defense

Things and people with bad intentions that enter your Cipher must be pushed out.

34

Engagement

Prey passes the lion who,

Sometimes merely looks,

Sometimes pounces without hesitation,

However never fails to act.

35

Utilization

Kites harness the force of the wind.

They express our intentions,

But they cannot change the wind..

36

Vantage

Distant ridges, far away clouds,

All events come from distance.

With a high vantage point,

Foretelling the future is elementary.

37

Discord

When birds fly too high

They sing out of tune.

38

Adapting

Heaven embraces the horizon,

No matter how jagged the profile

The sky faithfully conforms.

39

Worry

Worry is an addiction

It interferes with compassion.

Subconscious

Heaven and hell:

Our subconscious.

41

Resolution

Footsteps in the sand

Quickly washed away:

The seashore's mind.

42

Walking

Trail beside stream,

Fragrant pine.

Rocky red earth,

Steep Mountain.

43

Perseverance

Invisible lines.

The angler repairs his net

And the fish are nearly caught.

44

Stretching

When young, things are soft

When old things are brittle.

45

Circulation

Spirituality begins in the loins

Ascends up the back,

And returns to the navel.

46

Organization

Pattern and creativity

Are two poles of action.

Wusu Dumbuya Jr.

47

Impermanence

Tidal windstorm

Splits trees and rock,

Yet cannot last a day

So much less, man's work.

48

Knowledge

Life is

Beauty,

Terror,

And understanding.

49

Death

*D*eath is

The opposite

Of time.

50

Interaction

*W*e make life real

By the thoughts we project.

51

Beauty

Lavender roses,

Incarnate fragrance,

Priestly hue of dawn,

Spring unfolding.

52

Nonconformity

The world is dazzling,

I am dull,

Others strive for achievement,

I follow a lonely path.

53

Imbalance

Sleepless nights?

Diet, mind, conditions

Hold the possibility of correction.

54

Adversity

A tree hemmed by giants

Requires tenacity to survive.

55

Problems

Cannot be

Resolved at once.

Slowly untie knots,

Divide and conquer.

56

Muteness

The more you dwell in the spirit,

The farther you are from common ways.

If you want to speak of spiritual wonders,

Dissolve in your energy.

57

Predilection

Those who follow there heart do so

From their predilection.

There are no promises,

Yet the rewards are immeasurable.

58

Opportunity

The owl darting in the night.

Will you be able to see it?

Will you be able to capture it?

Cling to your heart like a shadow.

Move without a shadow.

59

Source

Wellspring of energy,

Rises in the body's core.

Tap it and be sustained,

Channel it and it will speak.

Celibacy

In winter, animals do not mate.

Preserve your energy,

By preserving your essence.

61

Sorrow

Rain scatters plum petals,

Weeping stains the earth.

One can only take shelter,

And wait for clearing.

62

Interpretation

All we can experience is subjective.

There is no sensation without interpretation.

We create the world and ourselves;

Only when we stop do we see the truth.

Articulation

Rain dropping from the eaves

Sound of nature's poetry.

We speak and write to explain our selves.

64

Unbound

Bird song flies unfettered

Over the blue sky and green fields

Once you feel the energy run

Give way, give way.

Accent

Chill morning, slick steps

The path to the temple is steep.

We may stumble at times,

But we must get up and try again.

Cycles

Dawn is shimmering of the horizon.

Dusk is settling of the sky.

Returning

Angels against lavender sky,

Flung across the heaven's vault.

Unfettered, swallows circle back to the nest.

68

Creativity

Storms break into pieces,

Clouds charge the horizon.

Revolving of the heavens

Generates all movement.

Illumination

Fire feeding on fire

Energy generating light.

70

Independence

A solitary crane

In a winter snowstorm

Needs no jewels.

Entertainment

The mind that turns ever outward

Will have no end to craving.

Only the mind turned inward

Will find a still-point of peace.

72

Discovery

Seize mountain spirits,

Make them divulge their secrets

Only with strength is there discovery

73

Affirmation

Stand at the precipice,

That existential darkness,

And call into the void:

It will surely answer.

74

Accumulation

An opening in the storming see,

Gold deposited on bones.

Once accumulation has begun

Take care not to interfere.

Breakthrough

Lake shadows color of cold,

Willow branches weep ice,

Swan rises dazzling in the sun.

Sanctity

Every soul is inviolable,

Any thought can be private.

The deepest goal is to

Find sanctity's source.

77

Fate

Dispel time and you will

Dispel fate.

Fear

Trust the gods within,

Accept given boons.

Illusion is reality's border:

Pearce fear to go beyond..

Spring

Sun and moon divide the sky,

Fragrance blooms on pear wood bones:

Earth awakens with a sigh.

Opposites

Before emptying, there must be fullness.

Before falling, there must be accent.

Before shrinking, there must be exploding.

To destroy something, lead it to its extreme.

To preserve something, keep to the middle.

Wusu Dumbuya Jr.

81

Openness

Nothing is meant to be

There is no predestination.

82

Attunement

Traversing sun leads to a new season,

Vernal breath attunes the leaves.

Parting

I and I assumed forever

When I and I became companions.

But now, unhappy, I are leaving.

The sky turns to bitter condolence

Un-slaked by resignation.

84

Intellect

Scholars, drunk on words and obscure meanings,

Weave tangled web of concordances.

Simple practice never occurs to them.

Give up modern education, and the world will be better.

Retrospective

You could labor ten years under a master

Trying to discern whether the teachings are true.

But all you might have learned is this:

One must live one's own life.

Images

Sound, smell, touch, sleep.

Can you think without clinging to these forms?

A thought without shape is hard to find.

Knowledge of one's energy is rarer still.

Integration

Be still to know the absolute

Be active to know the outer

The two spring from the same source,

All of life is a whole.

Interpretation

The sage whose words are ambiguous you call great.

Those who advocate discipline you shun.

With one, you treat words the way you want.

With the other, you resent having no quarter.

89

Disengagement

Wearily I open the prayer book,

Sepia photograph of sage and amber page,

Flaming raven Sanskrit, strange syllables,

Intone, chant, repeat.

Numbers vows with beads:

Every resolution is inspirational petrified.

90

Longevity

Contemplate in the morning.

Pull weeds from your heart in the afternoon.

The joys and labor of a single day

Are part of a whole journey.

91

Funeral

Even in death, we find no accord.

Accuracy

Every move count.

Pick your target and hit it.

Perfect concentration means,

Effortless flowing.

Confidence

Truth perceived gives assurance,

Skills yields self-reliance.

With courage, we can defy danger.

To increase power, increase humility.

94

Practice

Spiritual success is gained by daily cultivation.

If you practiced for the day, then you have won,

If you were lazy for the day, then you have lost.

95

Travel

Your body is a tabernacle.

Traveling one million miles,

The gods are still in place.

Constancy

Clear sunlight on the fallen snow: Fire and ice,

As bare boned trees shark the horizon.

Cold marshes, heavens geese.

A groundhog sits motionless on a post.

97

Truth

There are three levels of truth:

Experience, knowing, and reasoning.

All other assertions are rejected.

Farewell

We part at the crossroads,

You leave with your joys and problems,

I with mine remain, alone I took the road.

We must travel our own paths.

Homecoming

Where was my energy while I was gone?

Wasn't I following it where I went?

Do you think that we are separate?

100

Resolve

Banish uncertainty.

Affirm strength.

Hold resolve.

Expect death.

101

Gratitude

When you drink water,

Remember the source.

102

Clarity

Can you see sound?

Can you hear light?

Can you unite your senses?

Can you turn inward?

103

Redemption

I meditate daily before the alter

Yet I am covered with sin.

Acknowledgement

I would like to thank everyone who dedicated time

to read this book. I am grateful to have an audience

as graceful as you.

www.ingramcontent.com/pod-product-compliance
Lightning Source LLC
Chambersburg PA
CBHW042339150426
43195CB00006B/113